Dear Parent,

Sharing a book is the perfect opportunity to get close and cuddle with your child. Research has shown that reading aloud to and with your child is probably the single most important thing you can do to prepare him or her for success in school. When you share a book with your child, not only are you helping to strengthen his or her reading and vocabulary skills, you are also stimulating your child's curiosity, imagination and enthusiasm for reading.

Join Winnie the Pooh, Tigger, Piglet and all the friends from the Hundred-Acre Wood. These three delightful stories embrace the theme of friendship and encourage your child to think about the friends in his or her own life. Being able to connect to a story, by thinking about personal experiences that are similar, is an important strategy that enables readers to more fully understand and engage with the story.

Children learn in different ways and at different speeds. Remember, successful readers have one thing in common: supportive, loving adults who share books with them often, to nurture a lifelong love of books, reading and learning.

Enjoy your reading adventure together!

First published by Parragon in 2012
Parragon
Chartist House
15–17 Trim Street
Bath BA1 1HA, UK
www.parragon.com

Consultants: Cheryl Stroud, English Language Arts Curriculum Leader and Reading Specialist,
Concord Road Elementary School, Ardsley, NY; Beth Sycamore, Literacy Consultant, Chicago, IL

Editor: Joëlle Murphy

Designer: Scott Petrower

Illustrated by the Disney Storybook Artists

ISBN 978-1-78186-024-3

Printed in China

Friends

Bath · New York · Singapore · Hong Kong · Cologne · Delhi
Melbourne · Amsterdam · Johannesburg · Shenzhen

This is Piglet.

This is Tigger.

This is Eeyore.

This is Rabbit.

This is Owl.

This is Roo.

These are my friends.

Friendship Frames

Pooh loves looking at pictures of his friends! You can make friendship frames to hold photos of you and your friends.

Ask a grown-up to cut out this frame, following the dotted pink lines. Use a photo you have or take a new one.
A grown-up can help to cut the photo to fit. Glue in the photo and share it with your friends.

11

What Friends Do

We swing.

We paint.

We read.

We walk.

We bounce.

We hug.

We are friends.

Showtime!

Now create puppets to tell more stories about Pooh and his friends!

Ask a grown-up to cut out the pictures, following the dotted pink lines. Tape each picture to a lollipop stick and act out the many adventures of Pooh and his friends.

21

A Party for Pooh

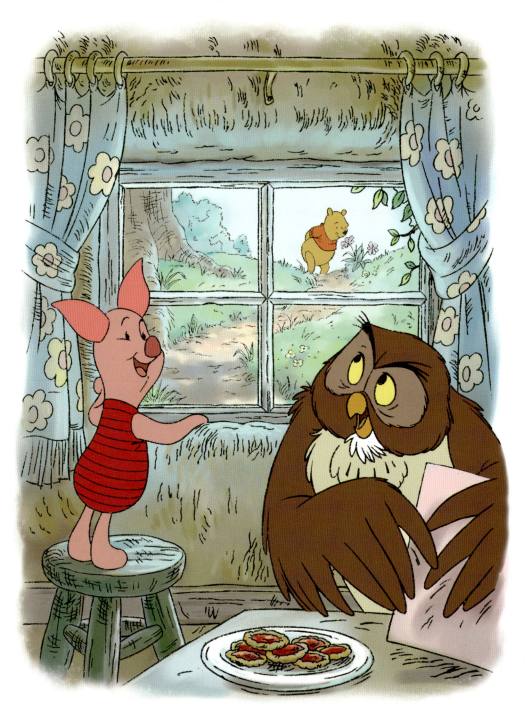

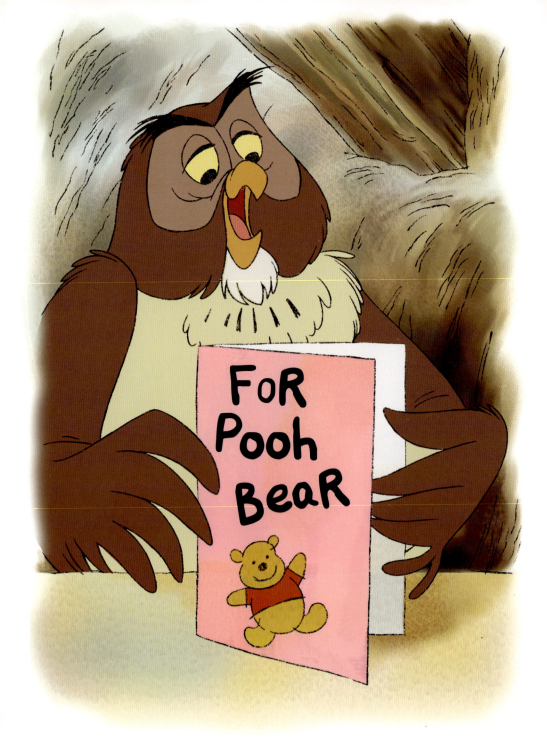

Here is a card.

Here is a hat.

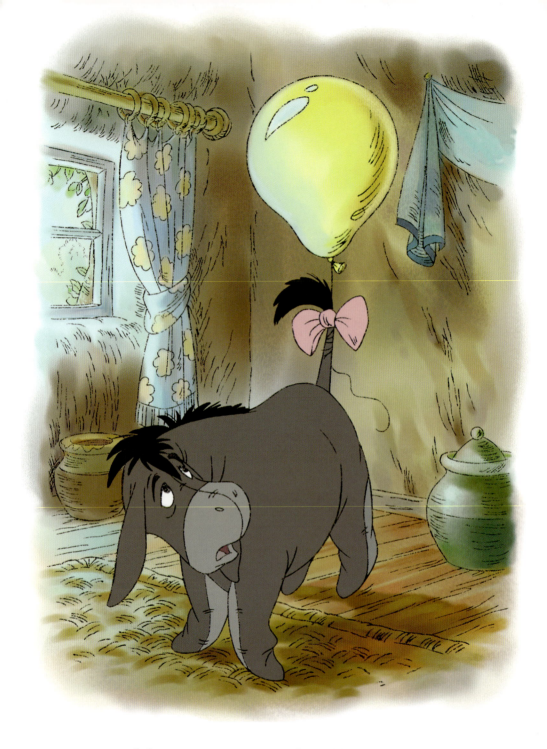

Here is a balloon.

Here is a cake.

Here is a present.

Here is a party.

SURPRISE!

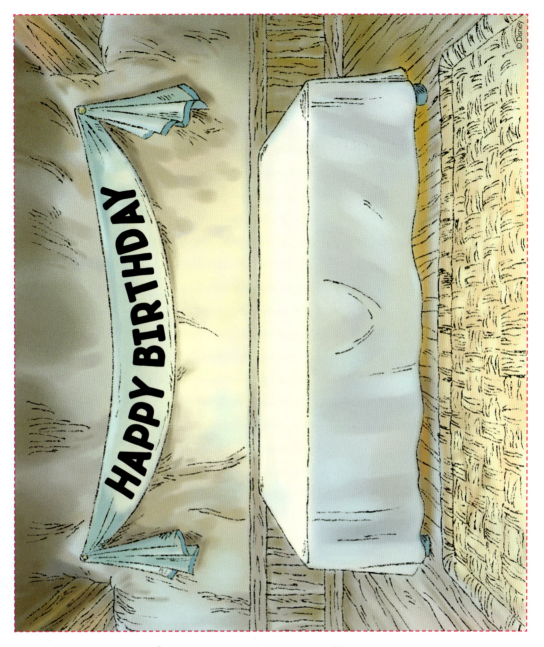

Storytelling Fun

Now it's *your* turn to be a storyteller. Use the picture above and the stickers found on your sticker sheet to help tell your own Winnie the Pooh stories.

Ask a grown-up to cut out the scene above, following the dotted pink lines. Place your stickers in the scene and point to the pictures as you tell the story of Pooh's party. Use more stickers and the scene on the back of this one to tell more stories about Pooh and his friends!